Everything You Need to Know About

HAVING AN ADDICTIVE PERSONALITY

Are you at risk for an addiction?

• THE NEED TO KNOW LIBRARY •

Everything You Need to Know About

HAVING AN ADDICTIVE PERSONALITY

Jay Bridgers

THE ROSEN PUBLISHING GROUP, INC.
NEW YORK

Published in 1998 by The Rosen Publishing Group, Inc.
29 East 21st Street, New York, NY 10010

First Edition
Copyright © 1998 by The Rosen Publishing Group, Inc.

Library of Congress Cataloging-in-Publication Data

Bridgers, Jay.
    Everything you need to know about having an addictive personality / Jay Bridgers.
      p.   cm. — (The need to know library)
    Includes bibliographical references and index.
    Summary: Discusses the nature of addictions to gambling, food, sex, alcohol, and other drugs, how they form and develop, their negative effects, and how to deal with them.
    ISBN 0-8239-2777-6
    1. Compulsive behavior—Juvenile literature. 2.Substance abuse—Juvenile literature. [1. Compulsive behavior. 2. Drug abuse.] United States—Juvenile literature. I. Title. II. Series.
    RC533.B74 1998
    616.86—dc21
                                                      98-8496
                                                           CIP
                                                           AC

Manufactured in the United States of America.

Contents

17.95

Introduction

Addiction is a relationship you have with an object (such as a drug or alcohol) or action (such as gambling or having sex). In an addictive relationship, you come to depend on that object or action to meet your emotional needs. For example, a person may eat compulsively to feel comfort, or gamble compulsively to ease loneliness. Often, you and the people around you don't even realize that an addiction has been formed. But as addiction progresses, it becomes hard to ignore.

All kinds of people suffer from addictions—young and old, from all walks of life. There are many ideas about why people become addicted. Some theories focus on biological causes, others on emotional causes, and still others on social causes. It isn't possible to explain addiction simply. But addicts do seem to have some common traits and go through a similar process in their addictions. When these factors are looked at together, they are often given the name "addictive personality."

In this book you will learn more about why and how people begin to form addictions. Chances are, you or someone you know suffers from an addiction, even though you may not realize it yet. You will also find out more about the many factors that have come to be known an addictive personality. Finally, if you are suf-feriung from an addiction, you will learn about where to turn to begin recovery.

The more you learn about addictions and how to stop them, the better you can live a safe and healthy life.

Addiction comes in many different forms.

Chapter 1

What Is Addiction?

Addiction is the compulsive need for a habit-forming substance or event. Though most often addictive relationships are formed with alcohol and drugs, they can also be formed with gambling, food, and sex. All of these things at first seem good for you because they have the ability to produce a positive, pleasurable mood change. But they also have the potential to be extremely harmful.

There are many stages leading up to addiction. It begins with experimentation, and then leads to casual use, compulsive use, and addiction. The progression from stage to stage can be very rapid.

In order to uncover more about addiction we must discuss its two forms, psychological addiction and physiological addiction.

Physiological and Psychological Addiction

Psychological addiction is coming to depend emotionally on the feeling a drug or action gives you. For instance, your craving for the sensations of smoking marijuana may lead you to adjust your life around getting high. When this occurs, your desire makes you feel that you can't live without it.

Physiological addiction goes beyond mental cravings. You know you are physiologically addicted to a substance when your body has a marked physical need for increasing doses. Drugs such as heroin, cocaine, nicotine, and alcohol all are physiologically addictive.

There are two signs of physiological addiction. The first is tolerance—the need to take more and more of a drug in order to get the same high. The second is withdrawal—the symptoms such as sweating, tremors, and tension that appear when you stop using the drug.

Different drugs are physiologically addictive for different reasons. There is no standard time for how long you must use a drug in order to become physiologically addicted to it. But once any addiction is formed, it is extremely harmful.

Why Get Started?

Many factors lead people into addictive relationships. They vary for different people.

Emotions

First, internal feelings such as stress, isolation, and lack of love can send you searching for relief. Often people turn to substances and compulsive actions as

Family stress can make you feel the need to escape through addictive behavior.

ways to escape from these difficult feelings. Many addictive relationships are ways to leave unpleasant emotions behind. But they give you a false sense of hope and security because they don't help you work through the source of your problem.

When you feel there is no other way to cope with your problems but through a relationship with a substance or action, then you could be on the road to an addictive relationship.

Social Pressures
Social pressures come from the external world and can spark and fuel addictive behavior. Learned behavior, socially accepted behaviors, and peer pressure are all

examples of social pressures.

We learn much of how to act and react through adults. When we are young, we are particularly vulnerable to their influence. This can be either positive or negative. But it's much harder to unlearn certain behavioral patterns than it is to learn them. If you grew up watching your father cope with his long work days by getting drunk, then you may have learned that that is the way to deal with stress. This can lead you to rely on drinking too, even if you know that there are more positive ways to deal with stress.

Family relationships are not the only way we learn things. Constant exposure to certain behavior in television shows, ads, and in the movies can lead people to experiment with—and become addicted to—certain drugs or behavior. For instance, if your favorite character in a movie is a big gambler who is always winning at the track, her "cool" lifestyle may lead you to gamble.

Peer pressure may also lead you into an addiction. We all want to fit in, and sometimes we end up doing things that go against our better judgment. No matter how much we don't want to admit it, we have all done things in order to be accepted. This is especially true when you're a teen, for you are often more insecure about being left out. You may, for example, have a certain group of friends who experiment with LSD. They may make you feel left out if you don't trip with them.

Addiction Affects Your Relationships

When you are suffering from addiction, you focus more on

If you drink alone, you are in danger of developing an addiction to alcohol.

the addiction than you do on others. You turn almost totally inward, isolating yourself from those people who can help. Unfortunately, the longer an addictive illness progresses, the less you feel you can turn to others. You begin to feel lonely and depend more on the addiction.

This has an effect on your relationships with your friends and family. Because addiction is an illness that isolates you, you begin to treat people as objects rather than individuals who have emotions and needs. People close to you can become fed up with being treated badly and may begin to keep a distance from you. In turn, you become even more isolated.

There is an emotional logic to why addiction becomes more important than people. You begin to crave the mood

Feeling lonely or left out may cause you to try something that leads to an addiction.

change caused by your addiction because it's predictable, dependable, and easily attained. People, on the other hand, may not always come through.

What Is an Addictive Personality?

There is no "right" way to characterize an addictive personality.

Some argue that an addictive personality is created from the illness of addiction. It is a change resulting from the addictive process that takes place within a person. The signs of change, such as depression, irritability, amd paranoia, emerge from the addictive process in the same way other long-term illnesses can change a person's personality.

Others argue that certain personality traits make some people more likely than others to develop an addiction. For example, people who are likely to try new things and take risks may experiment with habit-forming substances or actions. Other personality factors, such as low self-esteem and insecurity, also play a part in addiction—if you have little self-confidence, you may succumb to peer pressure.

All of these factors are important when you consider addiction. And however you define an addictive personality, it still has a great impact on people's lives.

Chapter 2

Common Addictions

To better understand how addiction works, it helps to know more about the most common things that people become addicted to. Let's look at some of the facts behind these particular addictions.

Gambling

"It started slowly," Heather said. "I began betting with friends in football pools and card games. I didn't always win, but I won more often than not. After a few months, I found I was betting all the time. I couldn't help it. I would skip school to go the racetrack or to the off-track betting houses. I can't begin to tell you how many lottery tickets I bought.

"My parents didn't notice at first. They were so wrapped up in work that they didn't realize I was taking money from their wallets. Some weeks, you know, I wouldn't have to steal from them because my winnings *would keep me going. But as time went on, I needed more and more money to bet.*

"One night I was so desperate I went into a convenience store. I'd found an old BB gun in my garage a couple of days earlier. It looked just like a real rifle. Anyway, I went into the store and held it up. The clerk opened the register without a problem. But he also pushed the alarm button without my knowing it. The cops were there in a second. Turns out the clerk only had twenty bucks anyway."

Now one of the fastest growing industries, legal gambling attracts more customers than basketball games or the movies. Many states depend on gambling taxes for revenue.

For most people, gambling is an enjoyable, social activity. But social pressures—friends, family, portrayals of big wins on TV and in movies, and ads for the lottery and gambling cruises—can contribute to gambling addiction. What begins as recreation can have devastating effects, especially because, unlike drugs and alcohol, it is not something most people think they have to be careful of.

Gambling has been called the "hidden illness" because it leaves no odor on the breath, no staggered steps, and no slurred speech. Yet people become preoccupied with it, spending hours thinking about past bets and planning the next one. As time goes on, the size of bets usually increases, and the person finds it very difficult to quit or cut back, especially while ahead. But losing can cause people to gamble even more than winning can, because the gambler is disappointed and frustrated. The only way the gambler can become happy is by winning the next bet, so he or she keeps on gambling.

The effects of gambling on individuals and on their friends and family are serious. Often, gamblers lose their jobs and destroy their careers, and many end up bankrupt. Families and friends become neglected while addicts spend hours at the tables or slot machines. Gambling can also lead addicts to steal or sell drugs to pay their debts.

Food

"I guess it started when I was about ten," Rob said. "I had trouble in school, reading, spelling, all that stuff. The kids in my class made fun of me, called me stupid and other names. I knew I wasn't stupid, but it still really hurt.

"I felt empty inside; no one ever invited me to their house. I was alone almost all the time. So I started eating. At first, it was just because I was bored. But then I found it made me feel better. It made the hollowness go away—at least, for a little while. Every time I started to feel unhappy, I'd eat. Soon, it seemed I was eating, or thinking about eating, all the time. When my parents would try to stop me, I'd sneak food into my room.

"I started to gain a lot of weight. People really made fun of me then. I mean, at thirteen I was two hundred

Eating compulsively often starts as a response to emotions such as anger, confusion, and loneliness.

and fifty pounds. School wasn't any better either. I'd been held back and couldn't seem to make any progress. I was miserable and felt completely alone.

"Then I found out I had dyslexia. I started going to a special after-school program. My grades got a lot better, and kids actually started coming to me for help with homework. But I wasn't comfrotable hanging out with them. I was just too self-conscious about being big. But I couldn't stop overeating, no matter how hard I tried."

Food is a common thing to abuse because it is easily available. Overeating, also called compulsive eating, usually begins slowly. Often, people have grown up overeating in childhood. This pattern then becomes more intense in adulthood. Eating becomes a physical way of trying to fill an emotional void such as loneliness. But overeating only causes a person to feel more isolated from others. He or she begins to think only about eating and often eats alone.

Overeating becomes habit-forming because a person's body becomes used to taking in a certain amount of food. Therefore, it can be physically as well as psychologically difficult to stop overeating.

People who overeat run into many problems if they do not get help. As they become more isolated, they forget about the people and things that are important to them. As a consequence, they run the risk of losing their jobs and relationships with friends and family.

There also is a physical consequence of overeating—becoming overweight. This often creates a feeling of shame, because many societies value thinness as a standard of beauty.

If someone becomes obese (severely overweight), overeating has physical consequences. Obesity puts a great strain on the body, especially the heart and lungs.

Sex

"I've always had kind of low self-esteem," Francis said. "I've never really felt much love from my parents. They both work all the time, and, well, my dad's an alcoholic. He's in AA now, but when I was really young he used to beat my mother. He even hit me a few times. So I guess I've always been looking for affection.

"I first had sex when I was sixteen. Physically, it didn't really feel that great. But emotionally I felt something I'd never felt before. It's hard to describe, but for the first time someone wanted to give me attention and affection. So my boyfriend and I started doing it all the time. I would feel so good, so sure of myself during sex. I'd make him skip class, and I'd sneak into his house at night. Every chance I had to be alone with him I'd put the moves on him. I really loved him, though, so it didn't seem like it was bad.

"But he wasn't enough. I started having sex with other boys on the side, inviting them over to my house, going to their cars at lunch time. I mean, I would have sex three or four times a day, sometimes with three or four different guys. I had to. I'd feel good while doing it, then gradually, I'd feel like the same old person, so I'd do it again.

If a person relies on sex as a way to communicate, he or she may cause strain in a relationship.

"But then I got pregnant from one of those guys. Usually, I would be careful, but sometimes I just didn't think about it. My parents flipped. They started asking around and found out what I'd been doing. For the first time, though, they started paying attention to me."

For many people, the unhealthy use of sex is a progressive process. It may have started slowly, but over a period of time their behavior progresses to increasingly dangerous levels.

Though researchers have not found any chemical or biological cause for sex addiction, they have found many possible psychological factors. These include having a low opinion of oneself, a need for escapism, difficulty coping with stress, and a memory of an intense "high" felt during sex.

Sex addictions can also be reinforced by constant exposure to sexual acts seen on TV and in movies and magazines. This doesn't mean that a person's actions can be blamed on the media. But this kind of exposure can create an environment that encourages unhealthy behavior.

As with other addictions, the problem escalates because of a person's powerlessness over a compulsive behavior. Sex, like gambling for the addictive gambler, preoccupies a person. It drives him or her to lie to friends and family, to have sex in strange places with strange people, and to continually seek out sexual encounters. Soon, the person feels out of control, experiencing a tremendous amount of pain and shame. However, this only serves to reinforce the addiction, because it's the only place he or she can find relief.

Often, a person addicted to sex loses relationships, experiences difficulties at work, is arrested, has financial troubles, becomes depressed, and can ultimately lose interest in things not sexual. He or she is also at a high risk of being infected with acquired immunodeficiency syndrome (AIDS) and other sexually transmitted diseases (STDs). The need for emotional release may be so overwhelming that he or she doesn't think about protection. Without seeking help, a person addicted to sex can lead a life of despair and potentially catch deadly diseases.

Alcoholism

"I've had kind of a rough life," Sofia said. "My younger sister died when I was ten and my parents divorced when I was thirteen. I haven't seen my father since, and my mom works two jobs. I guess I never really saw my father much when my parents were married, though. But Mom and I used to have a lot of fun, going shopping and to movies—you know, those kind of things. But that all changed. She didn't have time to be with me anymore, working and all. I kind of felt alone.

"So I began to hang out more with kids at school. I told them a little about my problems, but, you know, they weren't really that interested. I guess I should have talked to Mom—but anyway . . . All my friends were drinking, and they'd tell me how good it made them feel. I was fourteen then, and wanted to fit in. So I started, too.

"At first it was just a couple of beers every now and then. I liked the feeling. For the first time since my parents' divorce, I smiled and laughed. Drinking seemed to make me more alive. For the few hours I was drunk, I'd forget all about my dad leaving and Mom working so much.

"But after a while, I started drinking every day after school. Having a few beers or shots was the only way I could have fun. Slowly, it became kind of like the feeling I used to get when Mom and I would go to the movies together—all relaxed and warm, like nothing could ever go wrong.

"But drinking after school wasn't enough. I started drinking in the school parking lot during lunch. I'd even

Drinking with friends seems socially acceptable, but it can lead to alcoholism.

skip classes to go for a drink. For a while, it was cool. No one noticed. My grades dropped, but, you know, I could handle it. The teachers were oblivious. And Mom, she had no idea what was going on—at work before I got up, not back till I was long passed out.

"One day, though, my friends dared me to do five shots of whiskey one after the other. I was getting ready to go to Algebra, which I couldn't stand, so I chugged each shot they poured out. At first I didn't feel much. But then the hallway started spinning faster than it ever had before. I felt like I was on a roller coaster or something. As I stumbled down the hall to class, a teacher couldn't help but notice. The next thing I remember is throwing up in the principal's office with a horrible headache.

"They called Mom at work to come pick me up. I'd never seen her so angry. She was yelling like crazy, wondering why I had started drinking. I broke down crying. I told her I'd been drinking for over a year and that it was the only thing I could count on to make me happy. She was shocked. She said she had been so busy trying to make ends meet that she had forgotten to make time for me. She started blaming herself. But I told her it wasn't all her fault. I just started something I couldn't stop. I realize now that each time I had a beer, what I really wanted was to have the feeling I had when I was with her."

Alcohol is the most widely abused drug in the world. People have been using and abusing it for centuries.

Though technically a depressant (drug that slows down the nervous system), alcohol produces a drunken "high" that often allows people to forget the troubles they faced before drinking. When people are drunk, they often do or say things they would not do or say if they were sober. However, the high is short-lived. Often, when someone is "coming down," he or she feels even more depressed than before drinking. This only causes him or her to begin drinking again.

Alcohol also affects how the body works. When a person drinks all the time, his or her body adapts itself to having alcohol in the bloodstream and then comes to need it for stability. When alcohol in the bloodstream dips below a certain level, withdrawal symptoms begin. These can be as mild as a craving for alcohol, slight

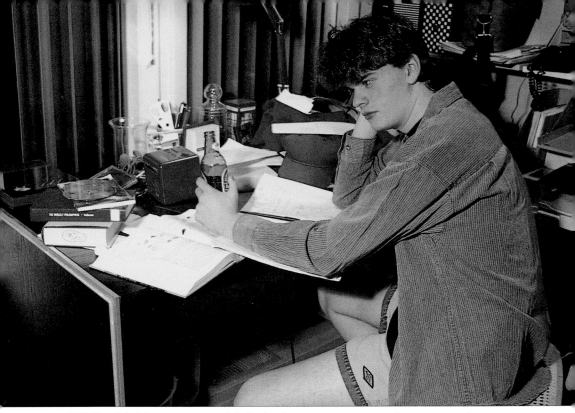

While drinking creates a high, it also creates an unpleasant crash.

tremors, and weakness. They can be as intense as vomiting, rapid heart rate, convulsions, and hallucinations. The easy way to fight these reactions is to have another drink. But that only keeps the cycle going.

Extreme cravings for alcohol can also result from genetic vulnerability. In fact, much research has been done on the possibility of a genetic predisposition to drinking. Alcoholism tends to run in families—studies show that about one-third of alcoholics have at least one parent with an alcohol problem. However, there is still much more to learn about a possible genetic link to alcoholism.

Many researchers also have found psychological factors that contribute to alcoholism. Not only do alcoholics become physically addicted to alcohol, they become psychologically dependent on it as well. There are several possible psychological factors. The first factor is failure in parental guidance. Unstable family environments can lead to poor decision-making in children, which can cause them to experiment with potentially harmful things. The second factor is psychological vulnerability. People who are depressed, stressed, tense, or feel an overall sense of unhappiness with their lives are often at higher risk of becoming alcoholic because they think alcohol can ease their problems.

There are also societal factors involved in drinking. Alcohol is widely accepted in our society. Although most people know that alcohol is addictive and that alcohol abuse has devastating effects, people still drink to unwind and have fun. Only when people become extreme in their drinking habits do others become concerned. At this point, it is too late for the person to quit drinking easily.

It is likely that a combination of factors leads to alcoholism. A person may begin drinking when he is depressed because he grew up watching his father do the same. Then, after a time, the body becomes dependent biologically on alcohol.

There are many prices to be paid for alcohol abuse. People's judgment is often impaired. Driving, riding a bike, swimming, and other activities are much more dangerous to people who are drunk. Alcohol makes them believe they can do or say anything. People who are drunk are not dangerous only to themselves. If they drive, have a weapon, or become angered, they can endanger many others.

Alcoholics face numerous health risks, such as damage to the heart, liver, kidneys, and brain. They also face psychological impairments, such as mood swings and memory damage. Also, alcoholism has devastating effects on the alcoholic's family and friends. It is almost certain that alcoholics will experience marital problems, broken social relationships, job loss, and financial problems. Alcoholics come to value their relationship with drinking more than anything else.

Drugs

"My parents both smoke pot," J.T. said. "One of my first memories is of them sitting at the coffee table with a bong. They tried to hide it from me as I grew up, but I knew. So when I was about thirteen, I started sneaking into their stash to get high. My friend Chuck and I would do it after school every now and then. My parents never knew.

"By the time I was in high school, I was smoking every day. I quit soccer and dropped out of the honors program because I just wanted to get high. My friends changed too. I started to hang out with all the stoners. One night I was at a club with some friends. I was coming down pretty bad, so I needed a pick-me-up. One of them had some cocaine, so I took a little bump. It was the best. I'd never felt so alive, such a rush. Later on that night, I did a little more, and then a little more the

next day. Pretty soon, I was buying it myself, doing it in the bathroom at school and on my breaks from work. I couldn't function without it.

"I thought I was handling it fine. But one night when I didn't have any money to buy more, I freaked out. I broke into the store where I worked. I knew the combination to the safe, so it wasn't a problem. The one thing I forgot was the video camera my boss had watching. I guess I had really lost it.

"The next day I woke up and the cops were at my door. I was in deep."

People start using drugs for many reasons, including curiosity, peer pressure, and the first pleasurable effects of the drug. Whatever the reason a person starts using drugs, it can very easily get out of control.

Following are descriptions of many drugs that people use.

Heroin

Heroin is a narcotic, made from the opium plant. It is an intense drug that causes an initial rush, then leads to a four- to six-hour high. During this high the user feels relaxed and euphoric. Following these high phases of heroin use comes a crash that produces a desire for more of the drug.

Using heroin results in a both a physiological and psychological craving for the drug. The time it takes for someone to become addicted to heroin varies, but on average, it takes continual use over a thirty-day period. Users then begin to feel physically ill when they have not taken the drug. Heroin users also develop a tolerance to the drug so that even larger doses are needed to get high.

When people addicted to heroin do not get a dose of the drug within eight hours after they come down, they experience withdrawal symptoms. Some people experience tearing eyes, chills, sweats, increased respiration and heart rate, and nausea. These effects can last up to three or four days. The severity of the withdrawal symptoms usually relates to the intensity of the addiction.

There are biological causes for these withdrawal symptoms. Researchers have studied the effects of heroin on the brain. They found specific brain cells into which heroin fits like a hand into a glove. The interaction between the drug and the brain cells apparently results in the drug's effects and may lead to addiction. But many unanswered questions remain for researchers who continue to study the biological causes of addiction.

We do know that there are other reasons for heroin addiction beyond biological causes. Many researchers believe that psychological and sociological factors are involved in the development of addiction. Though many people begin taking heroin as a form of recreation, most people usually begin because they need to escape from something in their lives.

Drug withdrawal affects both the mind and the body.

Many people who feel sad, neglected, or on the outskirts of society get hooked on heroin because it makes them forget their negative feelings. As they continue to use, they feel even farther away from the mainstream, usually joining other addicts to form a small network of "friends." Often, they abandon their studies or jobs and begin living only for their next high.

People are also drawn to heroin for the somewhat romantic hopes of a life on the edge. Watching and hearing actors and rock stars in their apparently glamorous lives, many people do not see the disturbances that lie underneath. They think drug use could give them a glimpse of a better life.

Biological needs for the drug, psychological addiction, and sociological reasoning combine to make a person believe that the drug is the only important thing in life. This makes it extremely hard for someone to get help and break an addiction.

Cocaine

Cocaine is a stimulant (drug that speeds up the mind and body) that comes from the coca plant. Like heroin, cocaine may be ingested by sniffing, swallowing, or injecting. Also like heroin, it causes a euphoric state for four to six hours, during which the user feels confident and content. Cocaine also causes headaches, dizziness, and restlessness. When it is used continually, psychotic symptoms such as hallucinations and paranoia may occur.

It is unclear how physically addictive cocaine is. In recent years, studies have demonstrated that abusers who quit "cold-turkey" develop depression-like symptoms. People who are quitting cocaine can also have memory and concentration problems. Though researchers have not been able to determine exactly what causes these reactions, they do know that cocaine, especially crack cocaine, is one of the most addictive drugs available.

The effects of cocaine on users is dramatic. Most long-term users have marked social problems, including family unrest, employment difficulties, and legal trouble. In some cases, cocaine use can even result in death, as was the case with college basketball great Len Bias, who died of an overdose in 1986. Many of these problems result from the amount of money users spend on the drug. It often costs thousands of dollars a year to support a habit, leading people to steal for drugs and neglect their families. Women who use cocaine while pregnant put their babies at great risk for both physical and mental problems. Often, babies of cocaine abusers are born addicted to the drug themselves.

Marijuana

Marijuana is a hallucinogen, a type of drug that causes the user to have hallucinations—see and feel things that aren't really there. It comes from the leaves of the cannabis plant and is usually smoked in the form of cigarettes or in pipes. Marijuana is related to a stronger drug, hashish, that is made from the resin of the cannabis plant, then made into a gummy substance. Like marijuana, hashish is usually smoked.

Though marijuana really gained popularity in the 1960's, it has been around for centuries; apparently it was known in ancient China.

Marijuana's effects vary greatly, depending on the quality and dosage of the drug, the personality and mood of the user, and the user's past experience with the drug. In general, however, a state of intoxication, known as being "high," results. Usually, people feel relaxed and a sensation of drifting, with senses being heightened. Often, a person's sense of time is distorted—an event lasting only a few minutes may feel like hours. Short-term memory may also be affected. You may walk into a room, completely forgetting the reason for being there. These effects are usually noticeable in minutes and may last up to four hours depending on the dosage.

However, marijuana often has other, more serious, effects. It may lead to unpleasant experiences. For instance, if someone uses the drug while feeling unhappy, angry, or frightened, marijuana may heighten those emotions leading to intense anxiety, depression, paranoia, panic attacks, even hallucinations and delusions. It often causes an increase in heart rate, slowing of reaction time, bloodshot eyes, dry mouth, and an increase in appetite. Marijuana also causes memory loss and a slowing of information processing.

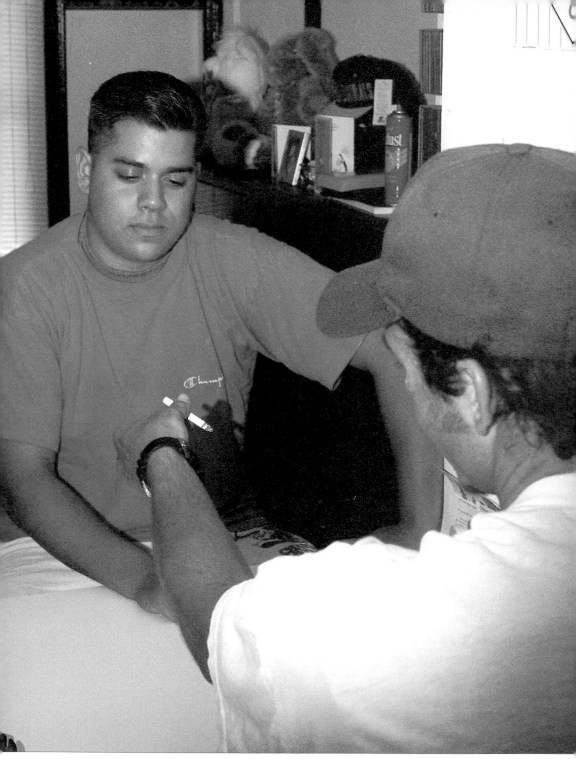

Saying no to peer pressure is the best way to avoid drug addiction.

Marijuana causes psychological dependence. There are also sociological reasons for continuing use. Marijuana is a fairly accepted and popular drug, and people use it to fit into the crowd. This psychological addiction and sociological reinforcement can make it very hard to quit using marijuana.

LSD

LSD (lysergic acid diethylamide) is the most potent hallucinogen. It is odorless, colorless, and tasteless, and can produce intoxication with an amount smaller than a grain of salt. Like marijuana, it is not physically addictive. However, its effects can be menacing.

After ingesting LSD, a people typically experience changes in sensory perception—that is, the way they see, think, and react to the world. This can include wide mood swings and feelings of detachment from their bodies. Often, their sense of time is distorted and they see things that are not really there. These feelings are commonly referred to as "tripping," for users feel as if they are going on a journey into parts of their mind (and the world) usually unavailable to them. However, there is no scientific evidence to support this. In fact, the "hallucinations" people claim to see under the influence of LSD are in fact just distortions of reality, not part of a created reality, caused by chemical reactions in the brain.

Experiences with LSD can be very traumatic. The distorted objects and sounds, strange colors, and new thoughts can be terrifying. People having bad trips have

Hallucinogens such as LSD cause frightening "trips."

been known to jump from buildings and set themselves on fire.

Despite the possibility of these negative consequences, LSD became popular in the 1960s for its supposed ability to "expand the mind." Many famous artists, writers, and musicians used, and continue to use, it as a way of influencing their creativity. But LSD has never been proven to push the artistic mind deeper. LSD remains fairly popular today as a recreational drug.

As mentioned, LSD is not physically addictive. However, people do psychologically crave the effects, and it can be difficult to quit, especially if you have never had a bad trip or known someone who had experienced one. The long-term consequences of LSD use are not known, though on occasion people experience a flashback, an involuntary recurrence of the distortions caused by the drug. Flashbacks can be very frightening, causing people to regret ever taking the drug.

Other Drugs That Are Abused

- Other depressants: China White, Special K. Depressants slow down your body functions, such as breathing and heart rate. They harm your ability to perceive the world around you and cause long-term damage to your liver and kidneys.

- Other hallucinogens: Peyote, magic mushrooms, mescaline, PCP (angel dust), and Ecstasy. Like LSD, they cause a hallucinogenic "trip." They can also cause permanent brain damage.

- Amphetamines: Amphetamine (speed), methamphetamine (ice, crystal meth, crank). These are synthetic (human-made) drugs that speed up the mind and body. They can cause permanent heart and brain damage.

- Inhalants: Household products containing solvents that are inhaled, producing a "head rush" or "high." They can cause organ damage and even instant death.

Chapter 3

Getting Hooked

Addiction to alcohol, drugs, food, gambling, or sex doesn't happen overnight. It's a gradual process. It's so gradual, in fact, that it may take a long time before you or others realize you're in danger.

The Stages of Addiction

Experimentation

Usually, someone begins using a drug, gambling. or having sex as an experiment. The reasons for experimenting range from wanting to escape from depression or stress to just wanting to have fun. The experimental stage is marked by doing something only a few times "just to see what it's like."

The dosage of drug or involvement with an event may be small or large, depending on the individual.

Regardless of the dosage, drugs can still be very harmful. It is very easy to overdose on heroin, cocaine, and LSD—especially the first time you try them.

Casual Use

Casual use is the next stage in addiction. This is marked by doing something only occasionally. Casual use is defined as a few times a month or less. Someone who drinks only on holidays is an example. Most people who casually use drugs or participate in events do so with small doses. Here, a relationship has been formed, but it is not yet a strong one.

Dependence

Dependence is a more intense phase of addiction. In this stage, the person does something on a regular basis. For instance, you may "depend" on a cocktail or two after work but still be able quit drinking without much difficulty. On the other hand, you may be a frequent user of cocaine and may have begun to feel you cannot live without it. Regardless of the level of dependence, it is not something to be taken lightly. It can lead easily to addiction.

Sometimes symptoms associated with addiction are present in the dependence stage, including increased tolerance levels and mild withdrawal symptoms. The effects on the body and personal life can also be more intense than in the casual stage. Not only can short-term problems occur, such as mild memory loss. But

Denying an addictive problem does not make it go away.

long-term problems emerge as well, such as financial problems for gamblers.

Addiction

Addiction is the final and most devastating step on the addictive ladder. It can be defined as an overwhelming compulsion for a substance or event on a continuous basis. The term addict is often used to describe someone who has this type of relationship with a substance or action. Addiction wrecks your life, including health, personal relationships, and job performance. Many people who suffer from addiction have shorter life expectancies, and there is a higher suicide rate among addicts, as well. The addiction becomes the

Addiction to gambling can cause someone to lose all of his or
her money.

most important thing in your life, even more important than your family. Job loss and unemployment are common.

How the Addiction Gains Control

Any problem with abuse or addiction is increased by denial. You don't recognize that the addiction is taking over, and you are beginning to lose control. The addictive gambler, for instance, may be able to acknowledge that she is spending too much time at the racetrack. She will try to justify her actions, saying "I got a good tip" or "I'm just gambling to unwind." No matter how many times she may be confronted about her problem, she denies that she has a problem.

Unfortunately, the more you deny you have a problem, the greater the problem becomes. Because you are able to justify your actions to yourself, you feel it is safe to continue your behavior. But it isn't safe. Before long, you will become completely focussed on the addiction. It will be very difficult for you to stop.

Although you can justify your actions, you still try to stop yourself. In fact, you continually fight with yourself about your addiction. However, you end up making up excuses for your behavior because you aren't able to. The high you feel is overwhelming.

You have fought and lost many of these internal battles. These losses only create more pain within you and cause you to seek relief in the addiction. The more fights the addiction wins, the stronger it becomes.

Out of Control

Once you are addicted, your behavior changes dramatically. You become completely consumed by the addiction and often seem to be a very different person. Your life revolves around your addiction—you skip work or school and ignore your normal responsibilities.

By this time, you have given up trying to understand what is going on. You no longer make up excuses for your actions. The addiction is almost the only thing you can think about.

The addiction becomes impossible for friends and family to ignore. It begins to cause a great deal of pain because trust and love are sacrificed for the addiction. Often, you betray yourself and others to hide your addiction.

The Results of Addiction

Once you are out of control, the results of your addiction can be overwhelming. Your life at this point has completely broken down. You begin to act in ways you never thought possible. Your behavior is so extreme that it can even scare you. Often your actions are even life-threatening. However, you are so dependent on your addiction that you cannot control your actions.

You can almost always count on losing your job or dropping out of school at this point, destroying everything you had worked for before the addiction. Your relationships with friends and family have also been severely hurt. Most times, friends and family have tried repeatedly to help you, only to be lied to or cheated.

Many people find it difficult to continue to help. It takes a lot of energy and great compassion to try to help someone who seems to be set on self-destruction. Most people do not have the strength to see you recover. That is why it's so important to recognize that you have an addiction and take the first step toward recovery. Talk to someone you trust—your parents or a friend's parents, a teacher or guidance counselor, coach, minister, or rabbi. They can assist you in getting the help you need.

Chapter 4

Family and Addiction

There is no clear evidence as to why some people develop addictions and others do not. For that reason, an addictive personality has many different aspects. Nearly all of them, however, involve a person's relationship with his or her family.

A Genetic Link

People have wondered whether there is a genetic trait passed on from parent to child that puts someone at higher risk for addiction. There is no evidence that addiction can be passed through a single gene. But studies have shown that children of addictive parents are far more likely to suffer from addiction. Studies on alcoholism, for instance, have found that the risk of alcoholism for children of alcoholics is three to four times that of children of non-alcoholic parents. While research like this does not point to one factor as the cause, it does help us understand who is at risk.

If someone in your family abused alcohol, you are at a higher risk for alcoholism.

If you grew up in a family in which at least one of your parents was addicted, you have a probability of developing an addiction. This does not mean that you will definitely develop a problem. But it does put you at a higher risk than children who grew up in normal households.

Learned Behavior

One of the principal reasons children develop addictions is learned behavior. A large part of how you act is determined by the way your parents act. You learn by watching and interacting with them. Unfortunately, people who are raised in addictive families learn addictive beliefs and addictive logic. For instance, if you had

an alcoholic parent, you learned that the way to cope
with a bad day was by having several drinks to numb
the pain. You grew up watching your parent drink every
day, hearing all the excuses the alcoholic gives for drinking too much. You think that this is normal behavior.
You may grow to adulthood knowing that this is not
right. But once the addictive logic has been learned, it
is very hard to forget.

Emotional Instability

The emotions within a family affected by addiction
shift daily. A parent addicted to drugs, for instance,
will be loving one minute and then, when he is high,
will be hostile or abusive. This can leave you feeling
unloved and can give you a false sense of a parent-
child relationship.

If you are from an addictive family, you may often
wonder where you stand in comparison to people outside your family. You grew up not knowing how a normal family functions. This leaves you feeling different
from your friends and can cause you to develop self-
doubt and become confused.

Because the love you receive from your parents is
very inconsistent, you may also feel unsure of the
world around you. You can have a difficult time trust-
ing other people and often expect the worst to happen.
For instance, you may fear that a relationship is going
to fall apart, even when there is no evidence of a problem. These feelings of doom come directly from living

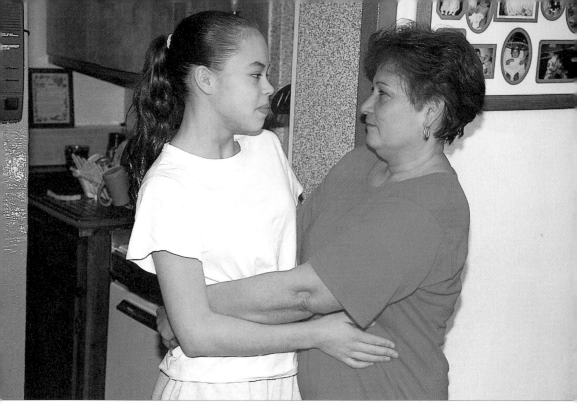

If you are suffering from an addiction, you may start to pull away from family and friends who care.

in a family where one minute things are fine and the next minute terrible. You probably were too young to realize that your parents' erratic behavior was caused by addiction.

Physical Abuse

Addiction in families can also lead to physical abuse. People who are addicted may treat others as objects, even beating or sexually abusing members of the family.

The families who experience this abuse suffer damage that can never be repaired. It leads to life-long emotional pain. Years after the abuse, many people are haunted by the question of why someone would do such horrible things.

If you grow up watching people communicate by fighting, you might believe that this is normal.

Unfortunately, children of abusive families learn the habits of abuse. They grow up seeing the lack of control of their addicted parent. Even if they know this horrible behavior is not normal, they may end up imitating it, for it is the way they were taught to act. In some cases, children of abusive families end up abusing others themselves.

Dealing with Addiction

Because living with someone who suffers from an addiction can be so traumatic, members of addictive families often look for ways to become numb to their problems at home. Children especially will do almost anything to avoid their unhappy home life. But this can be dangerous. Like the family member who has caused them so much pain, they can begin to believe that an object or action can make the pain go away. As we have seen before, this is the beginning of the addictive cycle.

It is best for family members to talk to counselors, teachers, or relatives outside the immediate family. Only through learning about the problem and talking about the emotions can a member of an addictive family truly find relief. Otherwise, the cycle will continue to be repeated.

Chapter 5

Recovery

"*These past few weeks haven't been easy,*" *Heather said. "The judge was cool, not making me go to jail. He understood that my problem wouldn't have been cured that way. So he's making me come here twice a week and attend Gamblers Anonymous two nights a week. It's nice being able to talk to people my own age about my problems. Getting things out in the open has helped. I wish I had learned to do it before all this happened to me.'*

Recovery from addiction is possible. But it takes a lot of work and patience. The goal of recovery is to break both the physiological and psychological aspects of addiction and take steps toward building a healthy life.

The First Step

The first step in recovery is admitting that there is a

If you have a problem with addiction, talk to someone you trust.

problem. You confront part of what you have been trying to ignore throughout the addictive process. Once you learn to be honest with yourself and trust others, you can learn to develop healthy relationships. Slowly, you begin depending less and less on the object or action that has consumed your life.

Support

Once you have admitted you have a problem, it is helpful to join a support group, enter counseling, or find another recovery program that suits your needs.

Support groups are made up of people who share the same kind of problem that you have. Many groups have therapists or counselors who lead it. Other support groups, such as twelve-step programs, are fellowships of people who share your problem. You help each other work through a course of recovery.

Support groups are helpful because you know that you are not alone. The group gives you encouragement to keep fighting your addiction. Because addiction can make you feel separated from the rest of the world, your involvement with others can restore lost self-confidence, making you feel like a complete person.

Counseling is another form of recovery that many people choose. You meet one-on-one with a therapist or counselor to talk about the addiction and its underlying causes. The more you talk, the better you come to know yourself. When issues come up, you and the therapist work on solving them together.

There are other options open to you, too. Many people choose to recover at clinics. Clinics can be ither inpatient (when you live there) or outpatient (when you come in during the day and go home at night). Especially if you are experiencing drug withdrawal, clinics will help keep you safe while you are recovering.

Recovery is a continual struggle. But it can be one of the most rewarding experiences of your life. It helps you learn how to trust others again. You come to understand the hows and whys of your addiction, and work out many of the problems you once tried to avoid through your addictive relationship. This knowledge can give you the power to confront your addictive desires when they appear.

Support groups help many teens overcome their addictions.

Through the recovery process you can begin to feel free. This freedom can be the most wonderful feeling you have ever experienced, one much more powerful than any drug or big win at the racetrack.

If you are suffering from addiction, please get help. Talk to a teacher, parent, counselor, or friend for guidance. In the back of the book, there is a list of places you can call to get the counseling you need.

Glossary

addiction Compulsive need for and use of a substance or action.

compulsive Having the effect of compelling a certain action.

dyslexia Failure of the ability to read or to use language.

genetic Having to do with the effects of heredity on a person.

hallucination Seeing or hearing things that do not exist in reality.

impairment Condition of damage to a physical or mental ability.

learned behavior Conduct developed by being exposed to it during childhood or youth.

paranoia Mental disturbance marked by notions of persecution.

physiological Pertaining to the functioning of the body.

preoccupied Mentally absorbed in a train of thought.

psychological Pertaining to the functioning of
the mind.
traumatic Causing stress or physical injury.
vulnerability Condition of being open to attack or
danger.

Where to Go for Help

Yellow Pages of Phone Book
Drug Abuse, Counseling, Gambling, Social Services

Drug and Alcohol Hotline
1-800252-6465

Prevention Crisis Hotline
1-800-9-FRIEND

Alcoholics Anonymous
A.A. World Services Inc.
P.O. Box 459
New York, NY 10163
(212) 870-3400
Web site: http:www.alcoholics-
    anonymous.org

Eating Disorders Awareness and Prevention, Inc.
603 Stewart Street, Suite 803
Seattle, WA 98101
(206) 382-3587
Web site: http://members.aol.com/edapinc

Gamblers Anonymous
P.O. Box 17173
Los Angeles, CA 90017
(213) 386-8789

Narcotics Anonymous
World Service Office
19737 Nordhoff Place
Chatsworth, CA 91311
(818) 773-9999
e-mail: wso@aol.com

National Institute on Drug Abuse (NIDA)
Public Information Department
5600 Fishers Lane, Room 1039A
Rockville, MD 20857
(800) 662-HELP
(301) 294-5401 fax
Web site: http://www.nida.nih.gov/
e-mail: information@www.nida.nih.gov

Overeaters Anonymous
World Service Office
6075 Zenith St. NE
Rio Rancho, NM 87124
(505) 891-4320
Web site: http://www.overeatersanonymous.org/

In Canada

Alcoholics Anonymous
#502, Intergroup Office
234 Enlington Ave. East
Toronto, ON M4P 1K5
416-487-5591

Alcohol and Drug Dependency Information and Counseling Services
#2, 2471 1/2 Portage Ave
Winnipeg, MB R3J 0N6
204-831-1999

For Further Reading

Banfield, Susan. *Inside Recovery: How the Twelve Step Program Can Work for You.* New York: The Rosen Publishing Group, 1998

Fanning, Patrick. *The Addiction Workbook.* Oakland: New Harbinger, 1997.

Klein, Wendy. *Drugs and Denial.* New York: The Rosen Publishing Group, 1998

McKoy, Kathy, and Charles Wibbelsman, MD. *Life Happens: A Teenager's Guide to Friends, Failure, Sexuality, Love, Rejection, Addiction, Peer Pressure, Families, Loss, Depression, and Change.* New York: Perigree, 1996.

Nakken, Craig. *The Addictive Personality.* Center City, MN: Hazelden, 1996.

Ward, Christie. *Compulsive Eating: The Struggle to Feed the Hunger Inside.* New York: The Rosen Publishing Group, 1998.

Index

About The Author

Jay Bridgers directed direct-mail book clubs for several years. He currently is a freelance writer.

Photo Credits

Photo on p. 8 by Michael Brandt; pgs. 11, 25, 36 by Kim Sonsky; p. 14 by Katie McClancy; pgs. 19, 38, 52 by Seth Dinnerman; p. 27 by Lauren Piperno; p. 55 by Ethan Zindler; All other photos by Ira Fox.